ME AND MY MUSE

HOW IT BEGAN AND HOW WILL IT END?

KEVIN GUYLO

ISBN 979-888530145-9

For Salad

Where's my love gone
Has anybody seen her
A loney Street
That's all I can see
Though she's walking away
Away away away

I've started to dwell on
the beauty of the first angelic rain
Turned into a lady of the lake
In love now
Who once was a rake

Contents

Contents

Preface

I am Kevin Guylo or you can call me DzikiZeke. Dziki means wild. That's how my life experiences have been, completely wild. If we're talking about me then it's impossible to not talk about my muse. Salad, like the beauty of the first angelic rain, she comes to me, touches me in a way I can't explain. In this book, you will find some poems and songs which might have meaning and some are just collection of words that don't really fit in this phyisical world, but, when rightly felt, can show you different sides of this life.

Hey

Come here, talk to me
I'm waiting here, for you
Someday, somewhere
You're gonna meet me
For now, let's experience the trip

1. A guy who feels low (Guylo)

The rising rage of the bloke,
making him sink
deep beneath the sea of fire,
still showing an urge to resist, striving,
might burn with pyre.

2. Experience the trip

Shaman shaman shaman
Have you seen her
She looks so fine like a fellow divine
I'm her fan and want to be her man
No way you can see her
What's in your head, you see
No way you can feel her
What's in you, you feel
Who she is, you will see
When you will jump into your very own space
Keep on flyin'
Keep on flyin'
Who's your hope one day you will find
Keep on flyin'
Keep on flyin'
Who's your hope one day you will find
Ride the waves
Taste the whole new world, you see
Don't hold a tree
This is just to set you free
Don't be afraid of the shadows you find
On your very own path

They will be your guides
Until you find your heart

3. A thought

Hiding away from the souls
in the corner, filled with dread.
Hankering for an inconspicuous piece,
glistening with love,
what others have just misread, shred.
Out of the blue, got divided
Left just a forlorn spot,
few clueless mortals
adoring illusive sprinkles,
unaware of the lonesome drought.

4. A painful loss

Before dawn a soul evanesced
in the endless sky
with clusters resembling spirits,
his loss sounded the death knell
of laughter and life;
felt an agonizing heat
nigh, burning pyre,
rising flames burnt the wire
of bond and love;
cried my soul out in the darkened, murky well.
Five years have passed,
since the parting day;
a hole, still alive
now, has become a part of me,
what once looked aberrant to me.
Began to despair of ever living
the ebullient moments again,
in dread,
with some tears to shed;
half dead man,
who crawled in the darkness,
now walking again,

but without a backbone,

though seems vile.

5. Her smile

Her smile after weeping,
like a rainbow after rain,
a beatific paradise
with a tinge of pain.

6. Nature is calling me

Nature is calling me
To lie in it's bed
The home of dead
Under the songbird's highway

7. Hidden voice

In an endless sky
with the freedom to fly,
desire of many not a few,
like an alp under sky
with hallowed peace,
only acquired by few.

8. Waiting For The Sea (A song)

Tryna be cool
while smoking some cigar
a lady walks inside the bar
with her hair sinuous like a valley
eyes shimmering like a star
Everything scattered
like gold dust in the storm
with a little heat inside
Vision so hazy
waiting for the sea
part him away from the stones
take him away

9. My Stolen Wine

Soft like sand;
a million faces in her realm
whisper in her ear,
sounds to me a sprightly paean,
when I ask them to tell me she's near.
Her steps sound so clear
explaining the very true,
a sentient being
in the guise of me and you.
Rambles here and there,
in my mind, i hear her sing my favorite lines,
somewhere i see a painting of a fellow divine,
a rush seeps in,
and there i see my stolen wine.

10. Sad truth

On my way to somewhere I don't know
It seems like nature is crying,
trees standing with their heads down,
clouds look sad, watching us die;
There's complete silence on the highway,
birds flying high in the sky
whispering the spells leading to a tragic end
I can feel the connection
Everyone looks like a friend of mine
Poor men working for their lives
Rich busy building their empire
I see three guys on a bike
enjoying their ride
on the land of life
We all are same, we are humans
It's just that some got rich, some got poor
and some just got stuck in the middle
It's the reality
Come, let's enlighten our morality.

11. Night Of Darkness (A song)

There's some silence in the room
It might fade away soon
I have no concerns
It's just my soul that burns
Let the darkness stay
away from fake laugh's poison
Another day with no action
no bells or sirens
Just the sound of breeze making me sway
The room is filled with smoke
A burning cigarette in the hands of a bloke
Sheer away from the haunting whispers
of the people trying to get into your mind
unable to see or feel
This soulless mankind

12. Regret

Pain of living away from the ones
I loved, I cherished
Living life in pieces,
today with one, tomorrow with another,
never lived together.

13. First Meeting

In the wilderness of pain,
found shelter;
so compelling like the first angelic rain,
surrounded by dark clouds
together in silence,
desolated souls intertwined
immortalized each other in a poetic rhyme.

14. Dark Life

Gently falling down into the stifling well
endless stygian night
waiting for me to fall in it's crypt.
Gradually burying my eyes
with the image of an angel,
awaiting for me with a candlestick
to enliven my world.
Natheless with the pace I'm falling,
life is fleeting and hope seems to fade;
The end is awaiting
Natheless thou cannot evade.

15. Trip to somewhere I

On our way to somewhere,
guards blocking our way
in the city of crime.
Dirty river with life around
near the parallel tracks,
never ending buzz around
under the bridge of civilians.
A loner sitting unconscious,
but, conscious enough,
looking into space,
following the trace
of the ancestors
under the fathomless blue sky.

16. My friend

Innocent soul swimming
in the river of fear,
where many gave up,
died in suffocation,
hoping the end is not near.

17. Dream I Regret

Pall of silence over my head,
In despair, wildered, like an almost dead,
Unmapped street hauling
Manifesting the mystique crawling.
Flickering flame o'er my skin,
A thousand pins slinking in,
I saw a hazy shadow fluttering near,
Mitigating the pain.
Her blissful smile,
In the guise of an angel of paradise,
Standing next to me,
Who was she?
Burn me burn me burn me
Like a crazed wight I called
Baffled, bewildered, mystified
Was her silence,
Busy playing her own wicked games, I bawled.
But she evanesced like a droplet,
I hied down to the crossway
To sought the queer existence
Before fate glided to grey.

18. Let me go

It's time to go to a place
A place no one has seen before
A feeling no one has felt before
A state no one has touched before
Don't wait for me
Cause I won't come back
Don't look for me
Cause I won't be found
I'm going to be somewhere
You can't even imagine
So, it's better you just let me go

19. A poem of love

Her blissful chuckle, so sweet and serene
with soul of an infallible;
spellbinding, bewitching, enthralling
like an artistic marine.
An abode in a wild, deadly jungle,
a bonfire in snowy alps
showering the abiding warmth,
was she a fretful shadow of lies?
Or a light born soul saving lives.

20. It's Where I Belong

It's gonna be a long day
Walking down country lanes
With my bag and a guitar
Like a nomad wandering but the stage is far
Maybe it's where I belong
Under a tree
Or inside a cave
When the night is long

21. Dream Girl

There was a town burning
under the black clouds, yearning.
While dazzling fire looked immaculate
saw a girl dancing near, lost in her conscience,
reflecting her pale hands,
a perpetual image of pyre,
seemed like she owned the fire.

22. Christmas Tree (A song)

Christmas tree set me free
Voices carryin' above the sea
Of my past, lonely birds
Can't reach the fields ahead
standing scarecrows they see
Voices unheard
Christmas tree set me free
Lovers meet to reunite their love
Unaware of what's happening above
Nights are of sweet sounding bells
Days are spent hearing bagpipers, I yell
Christmas tree set me free
Roads look ugly bikers come and go
Riding their lives high when the nature is low
Trip goes on forever as it seems
Ender's game you will see, he deems

23. Morning Sun

Welcome to the country town
where streets glisten and people listen.
Two travelers confront
in this world were hidden.
Green tank asks the morning sun
to ask her to smile again,
when clouds hide
she looks across the wide sky
and finds a group of friends whispering
in through the wind of love.
He's shy and looks a little high,
she is a jewel with a tone like a cosy retreat,
watch two lives enlighten the world,
nature awaits while the strangers speak.

24. Little Girl

I showed my wounds
and she cried too,
there was some magic we knew.
Riverside blues and stranger's booze,
for I felt so alone,
she rambled through the murky streets
hoping for one stranger's hand
and that's the life we've known

25. We

Silver space and open wounds,
startle him, she comes to him;
through the door,
leave the words, kept hidden,
when she tried, he lied
It's all forgiven
Spells and jewels
her sins, I fell;
extols the image
and the words she says
Her eyes my shore, the waves and cure;
night and light, my fear, my sight,
til spring to fall,
my dreams recall.

26. My only wish

I wish this pillow was your lap
and the ceiling was the sky;
your fingers touching my forehead
and my eyes in search of your smile.
I know the time would roll fast
if you and i were together;
stars would look to hide
in the blanket of the sunlight.
I would beg the stars to stay for a while
and i know they wouldn't deny,
when they would hear me say, to meet we've covered a million miles.

27. She lives in me

She's hides in the subtle nature of the wind
She lies in the hidden voices of the rain
From the light of the sun to the glitter from the stars
Comes through, she lives in me
She lives in you
Narrow streets and sweeping lanes
Crossroads and daisy train
River blue and fuzzy mane
Morning tea and growling pain
She lives in me
She lives in you
Stuck insane in the vision of sane
Slipped few times but managed again
She holds my hand from the sides you see
She lives in me
I live to see

28. So strong and true (Part I)

Shades and spades
A girl with braids
All live under one reflective roof
A spec of light seeps in through the bottom of the door
And she asks if this is the truth
In a muddle, she looks here and there
Everything crumbles and leads to nowhere
Fear of light and losing sight
A child's mind in fight or flight
Takes away what's there waiting to be seen
And yet it's unseen

29. So strong and true (Part II)

Hollow voices break the walls
Dust of words walks down the hall
And she gets scared as she wonders who's on call
Within lies a deep sense of truth
Pure, vibrant and strong
She questions if this is what she wants
When she hears from her roots
But denies to stroll down

30. So strong and true (Ultimate Truth)

Ride ride ride
Come fly in through the vast radiant waves
Or I'll meet you there at the end of the race

31. A river so kind

Bloodied in the river,
crossed a bridge, on it were two priests;
one resembled white, the other clothed in black;
saw me drown, a dog nearby,
one could see disappointment in his eyes.
Was carried away to the false end
by the river, I saw a whole new trend.

32. Let's disappear

Can't we disappear for sometime?
Some place where it's cold and white,
trees whisper their silence at night,
birds cover the sky in the shadow of our minds.
Let's go, witness the very best;
Before it ends, before we end,
and our world says the end.

33. Goodbye!

It's time to say goodbye;

goodbye to the illusional world,

goodbye to the aesthetic roles,

goodbye to the sordid souls.

34. Dreamland (A song)

She came to me on a sunday night
With a flower in her hair
And said will you be my guy
For our best until we're here
I said have you ever been this close to someone
Like the stars above still in the ocean
She said take a deep breath and hold my hand
I'll take you to our very own land
She came and sat next to me
And closed her eyes
Told me to feel her inner skies
And be one before we fly

Poet And His Muse

We will stay forever in these rhymes
Where is the poet and his muse?
This is the only place you can find.

Printed by Libri Plureos GmbH in Hamburg,
Germany